To the future of all our children.

FRIENDS at SCHOOL

by Rochelle Bunnett
Photographs by Matt Brown

STAR BRIGHT BOOKS
NEW YORK

We are friends at school.

I am Ryan.

I am
Annie.

We are
Shayne
and
Parker.

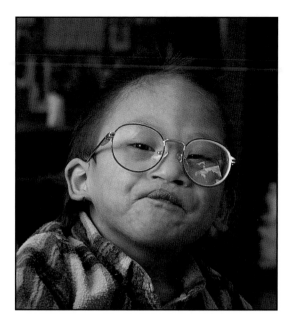

I am Chris.

We are Molly and Makenna.

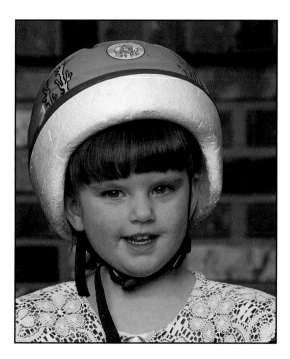

I am Shelby.

And
this is
Mocha.

7

Mocha lives at our school.
She loves carrots.
It's fun to feed her.

Mocha likes company. So we
keep her near us when we play.

Sam and Sara also live at our school. They are African spur tortoises. They eat all kinds of greens.

Every day there are special times when we can take Sam and Sara out of their terrarium and hold them.

There are lots of different things to do at our school.

We talk on the telephone.

We write letters and draw pictures.

We play counting games with a friend.

Our grocery store is always busy.

Ellie and Tyson wait in line while Elliott makes change.

Luka and Mario talk
quietly together.

Ellie puts on a puppet show.
Molly waits for her turn.

Nikko reads a story to Ellie and Dash.

Molly doesn't use a book to tell a story.
She just makes one up as she goes along.

Molly knows lots of songs
and teaches them to us.

Puzzles
are fun.

We like to do
them on our
own. But if a
friend helps,
that's fun, too.

Everyone likes playing in the water tub. Look at what's in the tub today.
There's blue flubber and whales! Flubber feels cold and gooey when you squeeze it.

Some days we put cornmeal or sand into the tub instead of water.

Everyone has a job to do at cleanup time.

Splash and scrub. Chris and Molly wash their hands with warm soapy water at the sink.

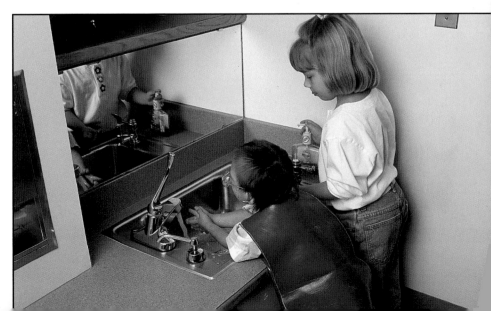

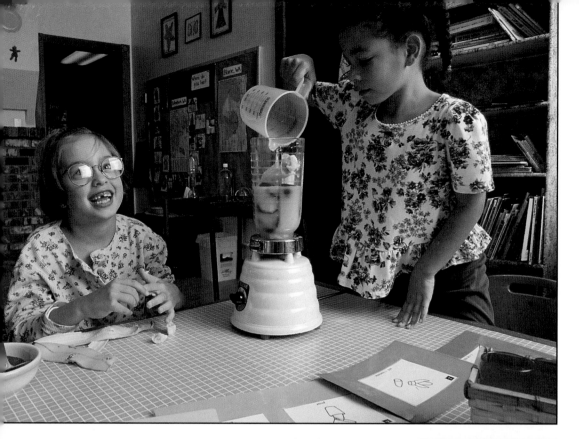

Snack time.

We make "moo-shakes."
Here's how we do it:
We put strawberries,
peeled bananas, one cup
of orange juice, and one
cup of milk into the
blender.

Don't forget to
put the lid back
on the container!

Shayne presses
the button—
vrrooomm.

Chris pours some for everyone. Mmmmmm. It tastes good.
Sometimes we get "moo-staches" from drinking "moo-shakes."

At our school we play
outside all year round.

Here are some
of the things we
like to do outside.

Go fast or slow,
forward, backward,
high and low
on the swings.

Make mud pies in the sandbox.

We play on the
slide.

Ryan hears someone
coming down the slide.
Who can it be?

It's Annie!

We play a circle game together.

Or play with one special friend.

Our school goes on field trips.

In fall we go to Happy Valley Pumpkin Farm.

When we get back to school we scoop out the pumpkin seeds and bake them.

Sometimes we go by bus.

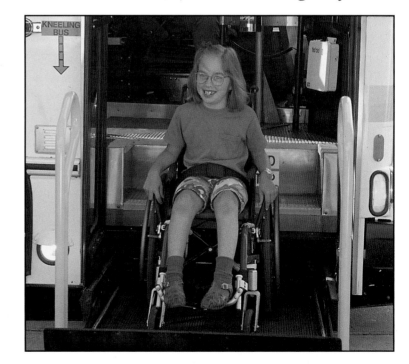

We visit the fire station.

Everyone likes painting
on an easel.

But painting the fence
at school is much
more fun.

Schooltime is over. It's time to go home.

Shelby puts on her coat.
Maura puts on her boots.

Good-bye, everyone. We hope to see you soon!

MEET THE FRIENDS AT SCHOOL

ANNIE likes to play card games, draw pictures, and make up silly songs. She is learning to snap her fingers, memorize her phone number, and ride a two-wheel bicycle. Appears on pages: cover, 6, 10, 11, 15, 20, 22, 23, 24.

BRITTANY likes to play with her dolls and write stories. She is learning to sew on a sewing machine and to cartwheel. Brittany is a student helper. Appears on pages: 8, 9, 20, 23.

CHRIS likes to play with puppets, to sing, and to learn new sign words. He is learning to put on his shoes. Chris was born with Down's syndrome and a heart defect. Appears on pages: 7, 14, 17, 19, 21, 25.

DASH likes to go crabbing with his dad and play pretend pet store. He is learning to ski down hill, floss his teeth, and draw pictures. Appears on pages: cover, title page, 14, 16, 24, 27.

ELLIE likes to go to the park and visit the animals at the zoo. She is learning to play hopscotch and spell her first name. Appears on pages: 12, 13, 14, 17.

ELLIOT likes to dribble a basketball and do jigsaw puzzles with lots of pieces. He is learning to call friends on the telephone and to write letters and numbers. Elliott has attention deficit hyper activity disorder. Appears on pages: 12, 17, 20.

KATIE likes to tell stories into the tape recorder and have friends over to visit. She is learning to zip her own coat and tie her own shoes. Appears on pages: 14, 20, 21, 24.

LAURA likes to read stories to her friends and play the piano. She is learning to ride a horse and do multiplication tables. Laura has a hearing loss and wears a hearing aid. Laura is a student helper. Appears on pages: 10, 23.

LUKA likes to play in the garden and ski fast downhill. She is learning how to make a cherry pie and ride her two-wheel bike. Appears on pages: 8, 10, 13, 14, 19, 23.

MAKENNA likes to play games on the computer and to read stories. She is learning to cartwheel and to use the telephone book. Makenna was born with cerebral palsy. Appears on pages: cover, 7, 14, 15, 18, 20, 24.

MARIO likes to bake oatmeal cookies and ask "why" questions. He is learning to play hockey and to ride his trike. Appears on pages: cover, 8, 13, 23, 24, 25.

MAURA likes to sing, eat strawberries, and play house. She is learning to brush her teeth, jump rope, and read. Appears on pages: title page, 16, 20, 26, 27.

MOLLY likes to be with her friends at school, do art projects, and read. She is learning to sign the ABCs and tie her shoes. Appears on pages: 7, 10, 13, 14, 16, 17, 20, 23.

NIKKO likes to draw, play soccer, and cook spicy dishes. He likes learning math tricks. Appears on pages: cover, 14.

PARKER likes to ride his bike to the park, fish with his dad, and draw houses and suns. He is learning to whistle, swim in the deep water, and do headstands. Appears on pages: cover, 6, 10, 11, 20.

RYAN likes to listen to music and to eat banana pudding. He is learning to hop and jump with two feet and read his ABCs in Braille. Ryan was born blind and uses a cane to get around. Appears on pages: 6, 8, 9, 10, 20, 22.

SHAYNE likes to ride her two-wheel bike, go skiing, and play dress-up. She is learning to cartwheel, read, and finish projects. Appears on pages: 6, 9, 10, 14, 17, 18, 20, 21.

SHELBY likes to listen and dance to music, and play with purple playdough. She is learning to ride her bike and cut with scissors. Shelby was born with hydrocephalus. Appears on pages: cover, title page, 7, 12, 17, 25, 26, 27.

SYDNEY likes to play with blocks and go swimming. He is learning his letters and to write his name. Appears on pages: 16, 26, 27.

TYSON likes to have doughnuts with his dad on Saturday morning, play with his brothers, and draw pictures of animals. He is learning to swim, write his letters and numbers, and read. Appears on pages: cover, 12, 14, 17, 18, 19, 20, 24, 25.

MOCHA likes to eat carrots and to be held gently by a friend at school. Appears on pages: 7, 8, 17.

SAM AND SARA like to eat greens and sleep under the heat lamp. Appear on page 9.

The children in *Friends At School* have shared a little bit about what they enjoy doing and what new things they are still learning. What do you like to do with your friends? What new things do you want to learn?

❤ ❤ ❤
A WARM THANKS TO THE TEACHERS AND THE FAMILIES AND FRIENDS WHO ENTHUSIASTICALLY AND PATIENTLY PARTICIPATED IN THE MAKING OF THIS BOOK.